To my family whom I wrote these stories for
and my friend Lisa whom help me get started.

The Duncan Family

Avery's Day Of Helping

As Avery sleeps, Mom quietly opens the door. Wakes him up " Good morning" as she opens the curtains. Avery pops out of bed "Good morning Mommy" and gives her a hug. Mom says breakfast is ready, Pancakes. Avery says excitedly O boy my favorite!

Mom asks It's going to be warm out today would you like to wear the blue or green shorts? As they decide the clothes for Avery to wear for the day. She also lays out the rest of his clothes for him to put on after breakfast.

Avery met the rest of his family at the table. Dad gave him his orange juice and pancakes. His older siblings Will, Kelsey, and Jason ate quickly. They were meeting friends at the park, down the street. Avery asked Mom Can we go to the park too? Mom thought for a moment. "Yes, we have time" we have to go get some groceries after, their time at the park.

Dad asked dose anyone have homework, this weekend? Avery looked at the door. He put his backpack and Jacket by the door so he could find them Monday morning. Will, Jason, and Kelsey all together said NOPE!!

It was Saturday and only a few weeks of school, so there wasn't much work at all.

As the rest of the family were off to enjoy their Saturday. Avery announced he was done, with his plate. He put his and several of the dishes in the sink. Mom said Thank You for helping with the dishes. We will be able to get to the park sooner. Avery went to get dressed so they can go to the park.

When Avery and Mom got to the park, they picked a bench in the shade and sat down. From a bag, Mom pulled out 2 bottles of water and some apples for later.

On his way to the swings, Avery saw Mrs. Lee. Mrs. Lee had spilled some of the things out of her grocery bags when she sat them down to rest a moment.

Avery Stopped to help her pick up all the items, that fell out of the bag.

Thank you for helping me. Said Mrs. Lee, "You are such a big help." It has been a busy morning.

Avery smiles and replies you are welcome.
After saying goodbye, Avery was off to the swings. He found a few friends of his own. They tried to see who could swing the highest, as most kids do.

Mom and Avery decided it was time to have their snacks, Mom had cut up the apples. They ate and watched all the people coming and going in the park. They saved some of their water for the walk back, from the grocery store. So, they packed up and were on their way.

When they got to the market, Mom pushed the cart. Avery wished he could push the cart, but he was a little too short to do it safely. Instead, he picked up the Items they needed and gave them to Mom to put in the cart.

They talked on the way home about what to make for supper and drank the rest of their water. They decided on Pizza, after all, it will be a quick meal for a Saturday night.

When they got home Avery helped put away the groceries. He put the Items away on the lower shelves, that was harder for everyone else to do. Then put away the recycling bags in the closet by the door for next time.

Cereal
Soup
Cookies
Pizza sauce
Cheese
Dough

Avery brought his laundry to Mom so she could wash his laundry, while he picked up his room.

After he finished, he found Mom folding the towels.
She gave him a handful of wash clothes for him to fold.
Then some small towels.
Thanks for the extra help. We can get an early start on
the pizza dough started, for supper.

Pizza Dough
Pizza
Sauce

As Avery was setting the table, Will, Jason, Kelsey, and Dad all came home. They were excited to hear Pizza was for supper.   They all washed their hands and sat down to eat. Everyone talked about their day and ate till they were stuffed. Mom told everyone what a big help Avery was today.

Avery smiled and said, " I can still do big things to help even though I'm still little".

What can I do to help?

Who can use my help?

When is the best time to help?